The Nature and Science of

MUD

Jane Burton and Kim Taylor

W

FRANKLIN WATTS

NEW YORK • LONDON • SYDNEY

First published in 1997

Franklin Watts
96 Leonard Street
London EC2A 4RH

Franklin Watts Australia
14 Mars Road
Lane Cove
NSW 2066

Conceived, designed and produced by
White Cottage Children's Books
29 Lancaster Park
Richmond, Surrey TW10 6AB, England

Editor/Art Director: Treld Pelkey Bicknell

Educational Consultant: Jane Weaver

Scientific Advisor: Dr Jan Taylor

Set in Rockwell Light by R & B Creative Services

Originated by R & B Creative Services

Printed in Belgium

ISBN: 0 7496 2925 8

Dewey Decimal Classification Number: 553.6

A CIP catalogue record for this book is available
from the British Library

Contents

What is Mud?

Mud forms when soil is mixed with water. Soil is made up of grains of sand and dust that have been worn away from rocks. Soil also contains many little bits of dead plants and animals. This **organic** material in soil—called **humus**—is what makes it rich in food for plants and animals.

Soil can become mud when large animals trample in a rain pool. Sand grains, dust and humus from the soil become stirred into the water together. When the animals go away and the pool becomes still, the heavier sand grains sink to the bottom quickly. But the fine grains and humus may take several days to settle and form a layer of mud on top of the sand. The mud contains most of the humus that was in the soil and so it is rich in plant food, but the constant trampling stops any plants from growing around the pool.

Citrus Swallowtail and several **species** of white butterfly sometimes gather in swarms on the mud at the edge of pools where large animals come to drink. The butterflies flutter down to sip liquid food from the rich mud. ▼

◀

When large animals like these Eland and Impala come down to drink, they trample soil at the edge of the pool, making mud. The Marabou Storks in the background have already had a drink; now they stand around, resting and preening.

Mud by the Sea

Glasswort or Marsh Samphire grows where few other plants can live—on estuary mud flats.

A fast-flowing river is often loaded with soil that the rain has washed off the land. Further down river, the water flows less quickly and the sand it carries sinks to the bottom, forming sand banks. As a big river flows slowly into the sea, all that is left of the soil it carried is the fine **silt**. This gradually sinks to the bottom at the river **estuary** where the incoming tide stops the river flow twice each day, giving the silt time to settle to the bottom. Here, a thick layer of mud forms, sometimes building up into vast **mud flats**.

Mud flats not only provide food for birds but they are also a safe resting place for them. These Black-headed Gulls cannot be surprised by a fox because a land animal of that size would sink into the soft mud if it tried to walk on it.

The thick black mud of an estuary provides rich food for plants and animals. Here, Cord Grass is starting to grow in the mud, holding it together with its roots. Little spire shells are climbing up the grass out of the mud.

Estuary mud is especially rich and each square metre may contain many thousands of small creatures. Estuary mud is also good for plants. It is very **fertile** and special **maritime** plants start to grow in it. Their roots hold the mud together so that it cannot be washed away and, in time, it becomes land.

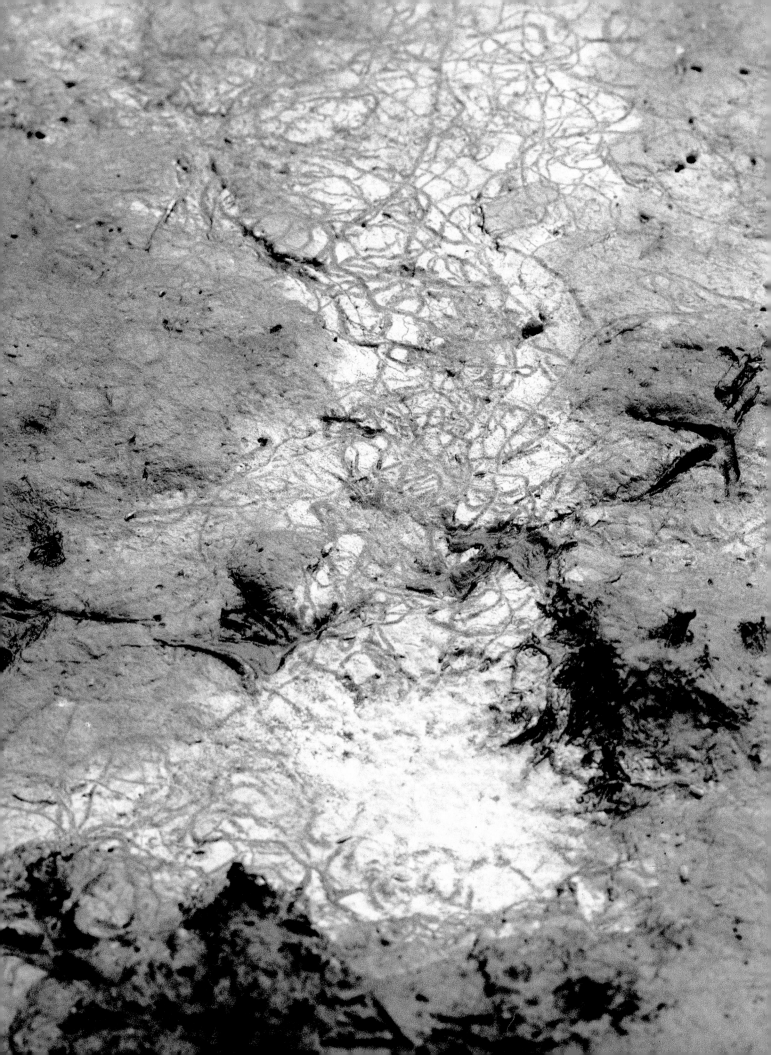

Smelly Mud

Mud is often black and smelly. It is black where plant material in it has rotted in the absence of **oxygen**. Only the top centimetre or two of mud contains oxygen—it is **aerobic**. Oxygen from air or water cannot reach the mud underneath and it becomes **anaerobic**. Anaerobic mud produces smelly gases including **hydrogen sulphide**. It also produces **methane**, sometimes called marsh gas. Natural gas, which comes from oil wells and is piped into houses for heating and cooking, is mostly methane and was probably formed in mud millions of years ago.

Only special kinds of animals can live in mud because there is so little oxygen in it. Most of these have to come to the surface of the mud to breathe.

◀ Here is some really smelly mud left when a pond dried out. A Moorhen has walked across it and left its tracks. Pond snails have also left tracks. The shiny area where the snails have been crawling is interesting because it shows faint colours caused by **bacteria**. It is the bacteria in mud that make the smelly gases – they are able to live without any oxygen at all.

▲
A worm cast of black mud shows where a lugworm is living in its burrow.

These mud-living **midge larvae** are red because their blood contains **haemoglobin**, just like our blood. Blood with haemoglobin is much better at absorbing oxygen than is the clear blood of other insect larvae. ▼

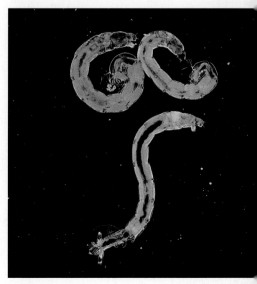

Mud-loving Trees

A male fiddler crab scuttles sideways. ▲

Mangrove trees also have other special roots that grow out from their trunks and then downwards, forming props to help support the trees in the soft mud. ▼

It seems unlikely that plants as big as trees could grow in soft, sticky mud—especially mud that is covered twice a day by sea water. But forests of **mangroves** grow on tropical mud flats. Some mangroves grow right down to the **low water mark**, showing only their tops when the tide is in.

Mangrove trees produce hundreds of spiky **aerial roots** which grow 10-30 centimetres upwards from beneath the mud. Aerial roots have many **lenticels** on their surfaces. These are tiny **pores** through which the roots breathe. Down in the mud, there is no oxygen and so mangroves need plenty of lenticels.

Amazing tree-climbing fishes called mudskippers live on the mud around mangrove trees. Some species of mudskipper grow to 15 centimetres or more, and they hop about over the mud after the tide has gone down. They use their front fins like legs and haul themselves up the aerial roots of the mangroves.

Mudskippers climb out of the water onto mangrove roots and onto mud. They display to each other by raising the fins on their backs like flags.

When the tide goes out beneath the mangroves, armies of fiddler crabs tip-toe out of their mud burrows. The male has one enormous, brightly coloured claw for signalling and for fighting with other males. His other claw is quite small and is used for putting mud into his mouth. The mud contains many organic particles which are good crab food. Female fiddlers do not have a big claw. Instead, they have two small claws and so can feed twice as quickly as males.

When the crabs sense that the tide is coming in, they return to their burrows. Just before the water laps over them, each crab seals itself in its burrow by closing the entrance with a neat plug of mud. A pocket of air trapped inside the burrow keeps the crab alive until the tide goes out again.

A muddy mangrove swamp is home to hordes of fiddler crabs which dig their burrows amongst the roots of the mangroves and come out to feed on the mud when the tide is down. The heron in the distance is probably looking for crabs to eat.

◀

The male fiddler crab waves his one huge claw in the air to warn other males away from his burrow. If they come too close, there may be a fight. ▼

The female fiddler crab has two small claws which she uses for scooping mud into her mouth. ▼

Foot-prints and Beak-marks

This sort of shrimp is found in estuaries. ▲

The organic material in mud provides food for shrimps, worms, snails and other animals which burrow in it. Vast numbers of birds often gather on mud flats to feast on these small creatures. Ducks have beaks that are specially good for dabbling on the surface of wet mud and finding all the small creatures that live there.

Many kinds of **waders** also feed on mud flats. There is a wader with the right length of beak to reach nearly every mud-dweller—from tiny birds with short beaks that pick shrimps and

A Shelduck swings its head from side to side leaving a regular pattern of beak marks on each side of its webbed footprints. ▼

Small waders, such as Dunlin, jab their beaks into the mud leaving rows of little holes. ▼

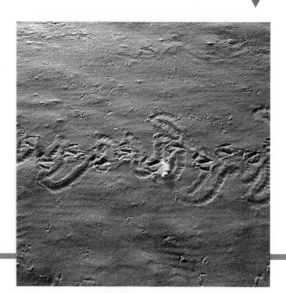

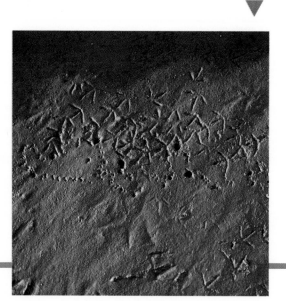

◀

Bar-tailed Godwits
are large waders with
slightly up-turned
beaks while Great
Knots are half their
size and have slightly
down-curved beaks.
They all have to wait
at the water's edge
until the tide goes
down so that they can
start feeding on the
mud flats.

snails off the surface to big birds with long beaks, straight or curved, that **probe** deep for worms and shellfish.

Birds feeding on mud flats leave a criss-cross pattern of three-toed footprints. There are round holes at intervals where their beaks have probed the mud. Ducks leave webbed footprints and a regular pattern of beak marks where they have dabbled. With practice, it is possible to tell what kind of bird has left which tracks.

Other animals also leave tracks in the mud. A mink leaves well-spaced five-toed footprints.

▼

A dog leaves footprints with four toes spaced around a central pad.

▼

Mud Nests

◀ Cliff Swallow nests are made of blobs of mud stuck onto the roof of a cave or the underside of a bridge. The swallows build a narrow tube at the nest entrance, just big enough for them to squeeze through.

Mud is used by many different kinds of animals to make nests or homes. When it is wet, mud is soft and **plastic** and can be made into shapes but, as it dries, it becomes hard, forming solid walls to protect a nest. Bits of plant fibre mixed with the mud make it even stronger, rather like iron **reinforcing** in concrete. Some animals mix **saliva** with mud which makes it set hard. **Termite** mounds are made of mud mixed with termite saliva. Some mounds are almost as hard as concrete when dry.

Some termite mud is so rich in **minerals** that Chimpanzees eat it as a medicine when they feel unwell.

Flamingos use mud to make their nests in a shallow part of a lake. They use their beaks to scoop mud into tall mounds. In a hollow on the top of the mound the female lays one white egg. The parent flamingos take it in turns to sit on the egg, to keep it warm until it hatches. The tall nests keep the eggs and the sitting birds clean and dry. The thick black smelly ooze all around them keeps them safe from enemies such as mongooses and jackals.

17

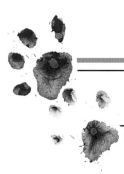

Mud Baths

Big cats and little cats may lie in wait near a water hole, knowing that animals come to drink.

You would think that mud is the last thing to use as a bath. People who get muddy have a bath to get rid of the mud. But some animals get into a mud bath because they *like* being muddy. They do this particularly in hot climates because mud is good for cooling the skin. A layer of wet

mud carries with it a lot of water and it is the **evaporation** of this water that cools them down. All the time the mud is slowly drying out, the animal's skin is being cooled. Water on its own would quickly dry and the animal would soon be hot again.

Animals that wallow in mud help to create permanent **water holes** from which other animals can drink. By trampling in rain pools, they stir up the mud which settles to the bottom later, forming a layer through which water cannot soak away.

This African Buffalo ▲ has been wallowing in red mud. Its horns and back are caked with it. While the mud is wet, it helps to keep the buffalo cool. When the mud eventually dries into hard lumps and falls off, it may take with it some of the **ticks** which plague the buffalo.

◄

Warthogs live in family groups. They roll right over in the wet mud so that their bodies are covered with it.

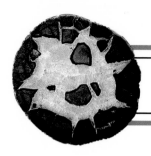

Mud Cracks

Over millions of years mud can become stone and the cracks in it become filled with crystals.

When a lake or puddle dries, it often leaves a layer of mud. As the mud itself starts to dry out, cracks appear in its surface. Sometimes the cracks divide up the mud into regular squares—almost as if paving stones have been laid. The reason for the cracks is that mud **contracts** as it dries. As water at the surface evaporates, the particles of mud try to move closer together to fill the space left by the water, creating **tension** in every direction. But the more the mud dries out, the less it is able to stretch and so it eventually breaks.

When a river dries out, the mud at the bottom is left exposed to the air. As the mud dries, it contracts and cracks form. Goats have walked in this mud while it was soft. Soon it will be hard and the goats' hooves will not sink in.

Mud cracks make different ▲ patterns according to the type of mud. Here, a thin top layer of mud has cracked into small flakes, while the thick layer of mud underneath has formed large slabs.

The speed at which mud dries ▲ affects the pattern of cracks. The faster it dries, the more it cracks, but the cracks are smaller.

The first cracks to form in a drying **mud pan** travel long distances across it. The next cracks form roughly at **right angles** to the first, producing a crazy-paving pattern. Once a crack appears, it goes on widening, and so the first cracks are wider than later cracks.

When mud dries right out, the tiny animals in it also dry out and die. But their eggs can survive and hatch out when they are wetted again.

Fossils in Mud

A lump of pale stone has been sliced in half and the cut surface polished. Embedded in the stone is part of a **plesiosaur** bone. You can still see the complicated pattern of the inside of the bone, even though it is now all made of stone. Below the bone, there is a shell, which has also been sliced.

Imagine a big, muddy river flowing down through a valley millions of years ago. A **dinosaur** falls into the river and drowns. Its body is carried down to a lake where it sinks to the bottom. In the dark depths of the lake, the body becomes a **skeleton** and the skeleton is covered by layer after layer of mud. The huge weight of mud on top of the skeleton squashes it flat and presses down on the lower layers of mud so hard that all the water is squeezed out. Gradually, the mud becomes stone, and the dinosaur skeleton becomes a **fossil** that is **embedded** in it.

Many other sorts of ancient animals have become fossilised in mud. But it is generally only the hard parts of these animals—their shells and skeletons—that remain. The soft parts of their bodies usually, but not always, rot away long before they become fossilised.

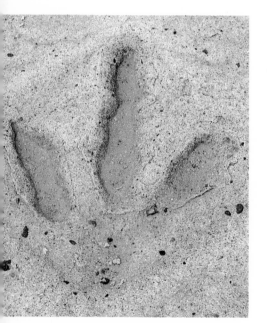

Soft things usually do not become fossilised but occasionally footprints in mud, like this dinosaur footprint, are turned to stone. Now we know the shape of the dinosaur's foot, not just its bones!

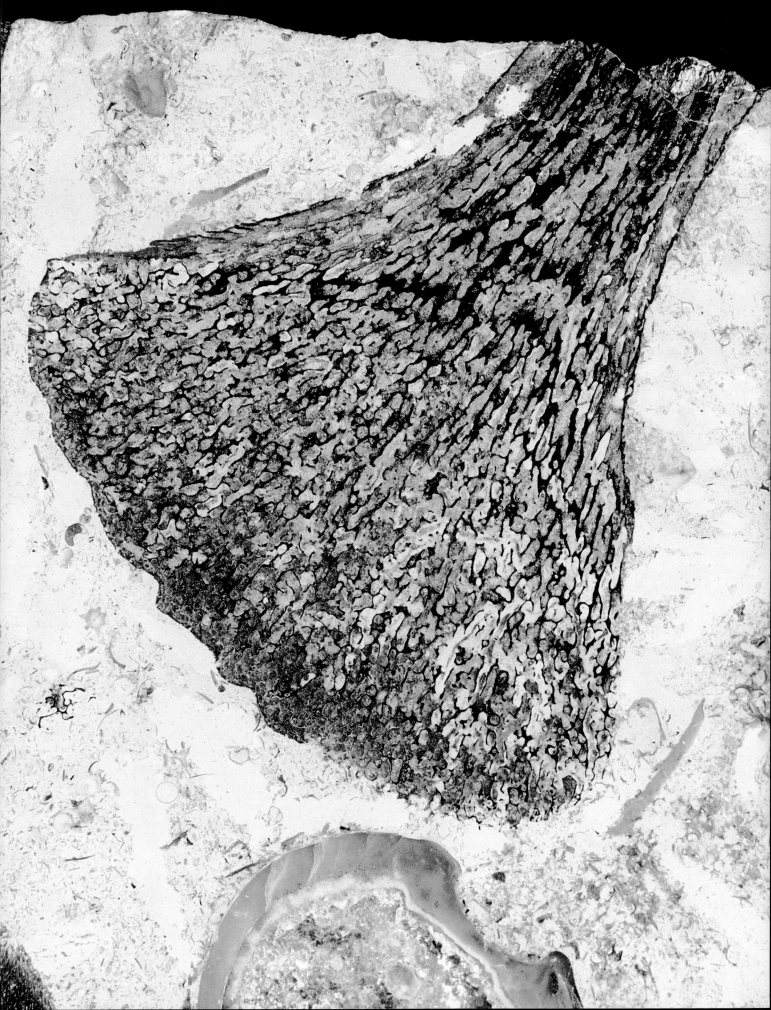

Mud is good for making fossils because it is fine and soft and fits closely around a dead plant or animal. If it were not for mud, we should probably never have known anything about life on Earth hundreds of millions of years ago. But from fossil bones, scientists have been able to work out what the animals looked like. We know from fossil teeth what the animals ate and, from fossil footprints, how they moved. Even nests of eggs and babies have been found, because these, too, can become fossilised if buried in the right sort of mud.

Ammonites had coiled shells rather like snails but the animals inside were more like octopuses. The shell on the right has been cut in half so that you can see how it was divided into compartments. The animal lived in the largest end compartment. There are no ammonites alive today. ▼

◀ Soft mud that was at the bottom of ancient seas has become a kind of flaky rock called **shale**. Some shale contains thousands of fossil **ammonites**. This large ammonite has been freshly exposed and gleams with **iridescent** colours.

Glorious Mud

A pumpkin seed  has started to grow in rich silt.

Mud is not like sunshine or air or water, which are things we cannot do without. Mud does not seem important, and people think of mud flats as wasteland. But mud *is* important—not only for the millions of tiny animals that live in it, but also for the birds that feed on them when the tide is out and for the fishes that feed there when the tide is in. Mud is also important for some of the very biggest animals, for cooling the skin and getting rid of ticks. Other animals eat mud as a medicine when they are ill. Mud is important for people too, because mud flats eventually become very fertile land. And mud carried by rivers fertilises fields in many parts of the world so that good crops can be grown. We *could* live without mud, but life would be much the poorer.

Mud that is carried ▶ down rivers may become spread over the land when the rivers overflow their banks. Mud is a natural fertiliser and makes the soil rich.

Hot water gushes out ▶ of the ground near some volcanoes. Occasionally it forms pools of boiling hot mud which bubble and hiss like a pan of thick porridge.

Things to Do:

Playing with Mud

Mud or Clay?

Most kinds of soil are made up of particles of many sizes—stones, pebbles, sand grains and fine dust. Mud is different because all the particles in it are much the same size and very small. This makes mud feel smooth and creamy when you rub it between your fingers. But there is another type of soil that feels very like mud. This is clay. Mud and clay are really much the same—the only difference is that mud usually contains organic material but clay is entirely mineral. Clay is formed of finely ground stone that has undergone chemical changes.

Baked Clay

Clay is interesting for experiments. You can either use normal pottery clay from a supplier or, if you are lucky, you can find your own clay. Clay deposits occur in many areas. They are nearly always in flat land and a sure clue to the presence of clay is a brickworks. This is because bricks are made from clay. The clay itself may be under only a few centimetres of soil and is often at the surface along tracks and streams where the top soil has been worn away. Collect a few lumps of clay and keep them moist by wrapping them in polythene. Natural clay is often yellow because it contains iron.

Before using natural clay, it is a good thing to take out any stones and bits of plant roots. Work the clay between your fingers to remove these lumps. When the clay is nice and smooth, try making a thumb pot. Form a ball of clay 4-5 centimetres across (**A**) and, with the ball on a flat surface, gently push your thumb down into it (**B**). As your thumb goes down, rotate the ball slowly, all the time pinching the clay between thumb and first finger to form the wall of the pot (**C**). If the clay starts to crack, use a little water to smooth it together again. You should be able to make a small bowl (**D**).

Leave your pot for several days to dry thoroughly (**E**). The clay is now hard but it is not water-resistant. If you try filling your pot with water, it will just crumble into a heap of mud! To become water-resistant, clay has to be fired. Heat produces chemical changes in clay which bind the particles together so that water cannot separate them. People made this discovery many thousands of years ago just by putting dry clay into a fire. Much the same chemical

A   B   C   D

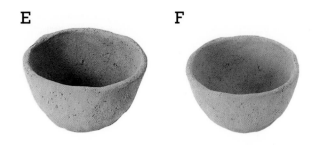

E   F

changes take place when mud stone is heated by volcanic action. It turns to hard stone.

Your pot should be fired in a proper pottery kiln. It has to be heated until it is red hot and you will need help from an adult to do this. When it has been fired and is cool again, the pot will be a different colour from the clay it was made from. Yellow clay turns to red pottery (**F**). Properly fired pottery is really hard and should ring like a bell when tapped. **Be warned:** *never put damp clay into a kiln or fire. Steam inside the clay may cause it to explode!*

Track records

Moist mud or clay is fine grained and plastic. This means that it is ideal for making **impressions**. When an animal walks across a soft mud pan, its feet leave perfect impressions, sometimes showing details of claws and even hair. But these footprints do not last for long. Rain, wind and sun soon smooth their edges, making them unclear.

To make permanent records of footprints, you must take plaster casts. For this you need plaster of Paris, water and an old bowl or metal can to mix them in. An old tablespoon is useful for stirring the plaster into the water. You will also need some strips of card about 3 centimetres wide, and paper clips.

A footprint for plaster casting should be recently made and clear. Surround it with a ring of card, clipped together to hold the plaster when you pour it in. Make the card ring big enough so that it leaves about 1 centimetre of mud around the footprint and push it a little way into the mud so that it stands firm. Pour enough water into the bowl to half fill the ring. (It takes a little practice to judge the right amount.) Gradually tip plaster into the water, stirring all the time, until it begins to look like soft whipped cream. Now quickly tip the creamy plaster into the ring and tap it gently so that the top settles level. (**Note:** *when mixing plaster of Paris, always tip the plaster into the water. Never try to stir water into dry plaster—it will start to set before you can do anything with it.*)

Plaster of Paris takes five or ten minutes to set. After this time, you can remove the cast and wash it gently in clean water. When the cast is dry, write on the top in pencil where you made it and the date. You should also write what kind of animal made the print. You can identify the cast by comparing it with pictures in books about tracks and traces or you could ask someone to help you. If you cannot find any natural tracks, it is quite nice to get your own pet cat or dog to walk across mud and to take casts of its footprints.

Glossary

Aerial roots: Roots that are in air rather than being in the ground.
Aerobic: Having plenty of oxygen.
Ammonites: Kinds of sea creatures with coiled shells that were very numerous 100 million years ago.
Anaerobic: Having no oxygen.

Bacteria: Minute creatures that are found almost everywhere on Earth. Singular: bacterium

Contract: To get smaller.

Dinosaurs: A group of animals that lived millions of years ago and were related to crocodiles and birds.

Embedded: Surrounded by or buried in.
Estuary: Where a river widens and flows out into a big lake or into the sea.
Evaporation: The change from liquid into vapour.

Fertile: Good for growing plants.
Fossil: Something that has been turned into stone.

Genus: The name given to a group of similar species. Plural: genera. The Large White Butterfly (*Pieris brassicae*) and the Small White Butterfly (*Pieris rapae*) are separate species in the same genus.

Haemoglobin: The red substance in blood which carries oxygen.
Humus: Dead plant material in soil.
Hydrogen sulphide: A gas that smells like rotten eggs. Chemical formula: H_2S.

Impression: The mark left by something that has been pressed into a softer material.
Iridescent: Rainbow colours produced by light striking very thin layers of clear material

Larva: A young stage in the growth of an insect. Plural: larvae.
Lenticel: A minute breathing hole in the skin of plant stems and roots.
Low water mark: The lowest line to which the tide falls.

Mangrove: Types of tree which grow in sea water.
Maritime: Growing beside the sea.
Methane: A gas made from hydrogen and carbon. Chemical formula: CH_4.
Mineral: Containing no organic material. Rocks are made of minerals.
Midge: A type of small flying insect.
Mud flats: Wide expanses of mud, particularly by the sea.
Mud pan: An area of mud surrounded by land.

Ooze: Soft, slimy mud.
Organic: Originating from animals or plants.

Oxygen: A gas forming about one-fifth of the air. Chemical symbol: O.

Plastic: Can be easily formed into shapes.
Plesiosaurs: Extinct swimming animals related to dinosaurs.
Pore: A tiny hole.
Probe: To search for with a pointed instrument.

Reinforce: To make stronger.
Right angle: The angle at the corner of a square or rectangle. Ninety degrees.

Saliva: Liquid produced in the mouth; spit.
Shale: Soft rock formed from layers of mud.
Silt: Fine particles suspended in or deposited from water.
Skeleton: The hard bony parts or tough outsides of an animal.
Species: A biologically distinct kind of animal or plant. Similar species are grouped into the same genus. The word species can be singular or plural.

Tension: Pulling action.
Termites: Pale-coloured insects that live together in nests built of mud.
Tick: An eight-legged creature that clings onto larger animals and sucks their blood.

Waders: Kinds of birds, usually with long legs and long beaks, that often wade in water to feed.
Water hole: A pool of water where large animals drink.

Plants and Animals

The *common names* of plants and animals vary from place to place. Their *scientific names*, based on Greek or Latin words, are the same the world over. Each kind of plant or animal has two scientific names—like a first name and a surname for a person—except that the names are placed the other way round. The name of the **genus**, or *generic name*, which is like a surname, always comes first and starts with a capital letter. The name of the **species**, or *specific name*, comes second and always begins with a small letter. In this book, capitals are used for the initial letters of common names to make it clear when a particular species is being referred to.

African Elephant (*Loxodonta africana*)—Africa **Cover**

Impala (*Aepyceros melampus*)—Africa 4

Eland (*Taurotragus oryx*)—Southern Africa 4

Marabou Stork (*Leptoptilos crumeniferus*)—Africa 4

Citrus Swallowtail Butterfly (*Papilio demodocus*)—Africa 5

White butterfly (not identified)—Africa 5

Glasswort or Marsh Samphire (*Salicornia*)—Eastern Atlantic coasts 6

Spire shell (*Hydrobia* species)—Eastern Atlantic coasts 7

Cord Grass (*Spartina* species)—Eastern Atlantic coasts 7

Moorhen (*Gallinula chloropus*)—Europe, Southern North America 8

Lugworm (*Arenicola* species)—Eastern Atlantic coasts 9

Non-biting midge (*Chironomus plumosus*)—Europe 9

Fiddler crab (*Uca* species)—Americas 10

Red Mangrove (*Rhizophora mangle*)—Americas 10,12

Mudskipper (*Periopthalmus barbarus*)—Australia, Africa, India, South Pacific 11

Fiddler crab (*Uca annulipes*), male—Southeast Asia 13

Fiddler crab (*Uca dessumieri*), female—Southeast Asia 13

Shrimp (Family: *Amphipoda*)—Atlantic coasts 14

Shelduck (*Tadorna tadorna*)—Europe, Asia 14

Dunlin (*Calidris alpina*)—worldwide 14

American Mink (*Mustela vison*)—North America, introduced elsewhere 15

Domestic dog (*Canis familiaris*)—worldwide 15, 29

Bar-tailed Godwit (*Limosa lapponica*)—worldwide 15

Great Knot (*Calidris tenuirostris*)—Asia, Australia 15

Lesser Flamingo (*Phoenicopterus minor*)—Eastern Africa and India 16

Termites (*Amitermes*)—Western Australia 17

Cliff Swallow (*Hirundo pyrrhonota*)—North America 17

Warthog (*Phacochoerus aethiopicus*)—Africa 18-19

African Buffalo (*Syncerus cafer*)—Africa 19

Domestic goat (*Capra hircus*)—worldwide 20

Plesiosaur (not identified)—Jurassic mudstone, Southern England 22

Dinosaur (*Megalosaurus broomensis*)—Northwest Australia 23

Ammonite (*Dactyliocerus commune*)—Jurassic clay, South England 24

Ammonite (not identified)—Jurassic clay, South England 25

Pumpkin (*Cucurbita pepo*)—cultivated worldwide 26

Index